AUTO MILEAGE LOG BOOK

Copyright 2014

MILEAGE LOG

VEHICLE: ________________________________

DATE	ODOMETER START	FROM	TO	ODOMETER END	TOTAL MILES

MILEAGE LOG

VEHICLE: _______________________________

DATE	ODOMETER START	FROM	TO	ODOMETER END	TOTAL MILES

MILEAGE LOG

VEHICLE: ______________________________

DATE	ODOMETER START	FROM	TO	ODOMETER END	TOTAL MILES

MILEAGE LOG

VEHICLE: ___________________________

DATE	ODOMETER START	FROM	TO	ODOMETER END	TOTAL MILES

MILEAGE LOG

VEHICLE: _______________________________

DATE	ODOMETER START	FROM	TO	ODOMETER END	TOTAL MILES

MILEAGE LOG

VEHICLE: ___________________________

DATE	ODOMETER START	FROM	TO	ODOMETER END	TOTAL MILES

MILEAGE LOG

VEHICLE: ___________________________

DATE	ODOMETER START	FROM	TO	ODOMETER END	TOTAL MILES

MILEAGE LOG

VEHICLE: ________________________________

DATE	ODOMETER START	FROM	TO	ODOMETER END	TOTAL MILES

MILEAGE LOG

VEHICLE: _______________________________

DATE	ODOMETER START	FROM	TO	ODOMETER END	TOTAL MILES

MILEAGE LOG

VEHICLE: _______________________________

DATE	ODOMETER START	FROM	TO	ODOMETER END	TOTAL MILES

MILEAGE LOG

VEHICLE: _______________________________

DATE	ODOMETER START	FROM	TO	ODOMETER END	TOTAL MILES

MILEAGE LOG

VEHICLE: ________________________

DATE	ODOMETER START	FROM	TO	ODOMETER END	TOTAL MILES

MILEAGE LOG

VEHICLE: ________________________

DATE	ODOMETER START	FROM	TO	ODOMETER END	TOTAL MILES

MILEAGE LOG

VEHICLE: _______________________________

DATE	ODOMETER START	FROM	TO	ODOMETER END	TOTAL MILES

MILEAGE LOG

VEHICLE: ___________________________

DATE	ODOMETER START	FROM	TO	ODOMETER END	TOTAL MILES

MILEAGE LOG

VEHICLE: _______________________________

DATE	ODOMETER START	FROM	TO	ODOMETER END	TOTAL MILES

MILEAGE LOG

VEHICLE: _______________________________

DATE	ODOMETER START	FROM	TO	ODOMETER END	TOTAL MILES

MILEAGE LOG

VEHICLE: _______________________________

DATE	ODOMETER START	FROM	TO	ODOMETER END	TOTAL MILES

MILEAGE LOG

VEHICLE: ___________________________

DATE	ODOMETER START	FROM	TO	ODOMETER END	TOTAL MILES

MILEAGE LOG

VEHICLE: _______________________________

DATE	ODOMETER START	FROM	TO	ODOMETER END	TOTAL MILES

MILEAGE LOG

VEHICLE: _______________________

DATE	ODOMETER START	FROM	TO	ODOMETER END	TOTAL MILES

MILEAGE LOG

VEHICLE: ______________________________

DATE	ODOMETER START	FROM	TO	ODOMETER END	TOTAL MILES

MILEAGE LOG

VEHICLE: ___________________________

DATE	ODOMETER START	FROM	TO	ODOMETER END	TOTAL MILES

MILEAGE LOG

VEHICLE: ___________________________

DATE	ODOMETER START	FROM	TO	ODOMETER END	TOTAL MILES

MILEAGE LOG

VEHICLE: ______________________________

DATE	ODOMETER START	FROM	TO	ODOMETER END	TOTAL MILES

MILEAGE LOG

VEHICLE: ___________________________

DATE	ODOMETER START	FROM	TO	ODOMETER END	TOTAL MILES

MILEAGE LOG

VEHICLE: ______________________________

DATE	ODOMETER START	FROM	TO	ODOMETER END	TOTAL MILES

MILEAGE LOG

VEHICLE: _______________________________

DATE	ODOMETER START	FROM	TO	ODOMETER END	TOTAL MILES

MILEAGE LOG

VEHICLE: _______________________________

DATE	ODOMETER START	FROM	TO	ODOMETER END	TOTAL MILES

MILEAGE LOG

VEHICLE: _______________________________

DATE	ODOMETER START	FROM	TO	ODOMETER END	TOTAL MILES

MILEAGE LOG

VEHICLE: ______________________________

DATE	ODOMETER START	FROM	TO	ODOMETER END	TOTAL MILES

MILEAGE LOG

VEHICLE: _______________________________

DATE	ODOMETER START	FROM	TO	ODOMETER END	TOTAL MILES

MILEAGE LOG

VEHICLE: _______________________

DATE	ODOMETER START	FROM	TO	ODOMETER END	TOTAL MILES

MILEAGE LOG

VEHICLE: _______________________________

DATE	ODOMETER START	FROM	TO	ODOMETER END	TOTAL MILES

MILEAGE LOG

VEHICLE: _______________________________

DATE	ODOMETER START	FROM	TO	ODOMETER END	TOTAL MILES

MILEAGE LOG

VEHICLE: ___________________________

DATE	ODOMETER START	FROM	TO	ODOMETER END	TOTAL MILES

MILEAGE LOG

VEHICLE: ________________________

DATE	ODOMETER START	FROM	TO	ODOMETER END	TOTAL MILES

MILEAGE LOG

VEHICLE: ___________________________

DATE	ODOMETER START	FROM	TO	ODOMETER END	TOTAL MILES

MILEAGE LOG

VEHICLE: _______________________________

DATE	ODOMETER START	FROM	TO	ODOMETER END	TOTAL MILES

MILEAGE LOG

VEHICLE: _______________________________

DATE	ODOMETER START	FROM	TO	ODOMETER END	TOTAL MILES

MILEAGE LOG

VEHICLE: _______________________________

DATE	ODOMETER START	FROM	TO	ODOMETER END	TOTAL MILES

MILEAGE LOG

VEHICLE: _______________________

DATE	ODOMETER START	FROM	TO	ODOMETER END	TOTAL MILES

MILEAGE LOG

VEHICLE: _______________________________

DATE	ODOMETER START	FROM	TO	ODOMETER END	TOTAL MILES

MILEAGE LOG

VEHICLE: _______________________________

DATE	ODOMETER START	FROM	TO	ODOMETER END	TOTAL MILES

MILEAGE LOG

VEHICLE: ______________________________

DATE	ODOMETER START	FROM	TO	ODOMETER END	TOTAL MILES

MILEAGE LOG

VEHICLE: ______________________________

DATE	ODOMETER START	FROM	TO	ODOMETER END	TOTAL MILES

MILEAGE LOG

VEHICLE: ________________________________

DATE	ODOMETER START	FROM	TO	ODOMETER END	TOTAL MILES

MILEAGE LOG

VEHICLE: _______________________________

DATE	ODOMETER START	FROM	TO	ODOMETER END	TOTAL MILES

MILEAGE LOG

VEHICLE: _______________________________

DATE	ODOMETER START	FROM	TO	ODOMETER END	TOTAL MILES

MILEAGE LOG

VEHICLE: _______________________________

DATE	ODOMETER START	FROM	TO	ODOMETER END	TOTAL MILES

MILEAGE LOG

VEHICLE: ___________________________

DATE	ODOMETER START	FROM	TO	ODOMETER END	TOTAL MILES

MILEAGE LOG

VEHICLE: ________________________________

DATE	ODOMETER START	FROM	TO	ODOMETER END	TOTAL MILES

MILEAGE LOG

VEHICLE: _______________________________

DATE	ODOMETER START	FROM	TO	ODOMETER END	TOTAL MILES

MILEAGE LOG

VEHICLE: _______________________________

DATE	ODOMETER START	FROM	TO	ODOMETER END	TOTAL MILES

MILEAGE LOG

VEHICLE: ___________________________

DATE	ODOMETER START	FROM	TO	ODOMETER END	TOTAL MILES

MILEAGE LOG

VEHICLE: ______________________________

DATE	ODOMETER START	FROM	TO	ODOMETER END	TOTAL MILES

MILEAGE LOG

VEHICLE: _______________________________

DATE	ODOMETER START	FROM	TO	ODOMETER END	TOTAL MILES

MILEAGE LOG

VEHICLE: _______________________________

DATE	ODOMETER START	FROM	TO	ODOMETER END	TOTAL MILES

MILEAGE LOG

VEHICLE: _______________________________

DATE	ODOMETER START	FROM	TO	ODOMETER END	TOTAL MILES

MILEAGE LOG

VEHICLE: _______________________________

DATE	ODOMETER START	FROM	TO	ODOMETER END	TOTAL MILES

MILEAGE LOG

VEHICLE: _______________________________

DATE	ODOMETER START	FROM	TO	ODOMETER END	TOTAL MILES

MILEAGE LOG

VEHICLE: _______________________________

DATE	ODOMETER START	FROM	TO	ODOMETER END	TOTAL MILES

MILEAGE LOG

VEHICLE: _______________________________

DATE	ODOMETER START	FROM	TO	ODOMETER END	TOTAL MILES

MILEAGE LOG

VEHICLE: _______________________________

DATE	ODOMETER START	FROM	TO	ODOMETER END	TOTAL MILES

MILEAGE LOG

VEHICLE: _________________________

DATE	ODOMETER START	FROM	TO	ODOMETER END	TOTAL MILES

MILEAGE LOG

VEHICLE: _______________________________

DATE	ODOMETER START	FROM	TO	ODOMETER END	TOTAL MILES

MILEAGE LOG

VEHICLE: _______________________

DATE	ODOMETER START	FROM	TO	ODOMETER END	TOTAL MILES

MILEAGE LOG

VEHICLE: _______________________

DATE	ODOMETER START	FROM	TO	ODOMETER END	TOTAL MILES

MILEAGE LOG

VEHICLE: ________________________

DATE	ODOMETER START	FROM	TO	ODOMETER END	TOTAL MILES

MILEAGE LOG

VEHICLE: _______________________

DATE	ODOMETER START	FROM	TO	ODOMETER END	TOTAL MILES

MILEAGE LOG

VEHICLE: ___________________________

DATE	ODOMETER START	FROM	TO	ODOMETER END	TOTAL MILES

MILEAGE LOG

VEHICLE: _______________________________

DATE	ODOMETER START	FROM	TO	ODOMETER END	TOTAL MILES

MILEAGE LOG

VEHICLE: _______________________________

DATE	ODOMETER START	FROM	TO	ODOMETER END	TOTAL MILES

MILEAGE LOG

VEHICLE: ______________________

DATE	ODOMETER START	FROM	TO	ODOMETER END	TOTAL MILES

MILEAGE LOG

VEHICLE: _______________________________

DATE	ODOMETER START	FROM	TO	ODOMETER END	TOTAL MILES

MILEAGE LOG

VEHICLE: _______________________________

DATE	ODOMETER START	FROM	TO	ODOMETER END	TOTAL MILES

MILEAGE LOG

VEHICLE: ________________________

DATE	ODOMETER START	FROM	TO	ODOMETER END	TOTAL MILES

MILEAGE LOG

VEHICLE: _______________________________

DATE	ODOMETER START	FROM	TO	ODOMETER END	TOTAL MILES

MILEAGE LOG

VEHICLE: _______________________________

DATE	ODOMETER START	FROM	TO	ODOMETER END	TOTAL MILES

MILEAGE LOG

VEHICLE: ___________________________

DATE	ODOMETER START	FROM	TO	ODOMETER END	TOTAL MILES

MILEAGE LOG

VEHICLE: _______________________

DATE	ODOMETER START	FROM	TO	ODOMETER END	TOTAL MILES

MILEAGE LOG

VEHICLE: ______________________________

DATE	ODOMETER START	FROM	TO	ODOMETER END	TOTAL MILES

MILEAGE LOG

VEHICLE: _______________________________

DATE	ODOMETER START	FROM	TO	ODOMETER END	TOTAL MILES

MILEAGE LOG

VEHICLE: _______________________________

DATE	ODOMETER START	FROM	TO	ODOMETER END	TOTAL MILES

MILEAGE LOG

VEHICLE: ________________________

DATE	ODOMETER START	FROM	TO	ODOMETER END	TOTAL MILES

MILEAGE LOG

VEHICLE: _______________________________

DATE	ODOMETER START	FROM	TO	ODOMETER END	TOTAL MILES

MILEAGE LOG

VEHICLE: _______________________________

DATE	ODOMETER START	FROM	TO	ODOMETER END	TOTAL MILES

MILEAGE LOG

VEHICLE: ___________________________

DATE	ODOMETER START	FROM	TO	ODOMETER END	TOTAL MILES

MILEAGE LOG

VEHICLE: _______________________________

DATE	ODOMETER START	FROM	TO	ODOMETER END	TOTAL MILES

MILEAGE LOG

VEHICLE: ________________________________

DATE	ODOMETER START	FROM	TO	ODOMETER END	TOTAL MILES

MILEAGE LOG

VEHICLE: ___________________________

DATE	ODOMETER START	FROM	TO	ODOMETER END	TOTAL MILES

MILEAGE LOG

VEHICLE: _______________________________

DATE	ODOMETER START	FROM	TO	ODOMETER END	TOTAL MILES

MILEAGE LOG

VEHICLE: _______________________

DATE	ODOMETER START	FROM	TO	ODOMETER END	TOTAL MILES

MILEAGE LOG

VEHICLE: _______________________________

DATE	ODOMETER START	FROM	TO	ODOMETER END	TOTAL MILES

MILEAGE LOG

VEHICLE: ________________________

DATE	ODOMETER START	FROM	TO	ODOMETER END	TOTAL MILES

MILEAGE LOG

VEHICLE: _______________________

DATE	ODOMETER START	FROM	TO	ODOMETER END	TOTAL MILES

MILEAGE LOG

VEHICLE: ___________________________

DATE	ODOMETER START	FROM	TO	ODOMETER END	TOTAL MILES

MILEAGE LOG

VEHICLE: ________________________

DATE	ODOMETER START	FROM	TO	ODOMETER END	TOTAL MILES